The
Chocolate Cake
Phenomenon

A more delicious way to minister

Ken Williams

ISBN:
9781489536723

DEDICATION

For Marcene, who for more years than I can remember,
has encouraged me to "write your book." She has recruited
friends, family, and associates to push me to finish.
Finally. It's finished.
Thank you for believing in me enough to relentlessly
hassle me.

CONTENTS

ACKNOWLEDGMENTS

A prompting when I was the Stake Young Men president taught me to pray for my stewardship by name every day.

As a Seminary teacher, I learned to recognize the voice of the Spirit.

As a father, I learned that my experiences can be duplicated and shared.

As a friend, I learned that I could make a difference.

Without the involvement of anyone at any stage of my experience, there would be no phenomenon. If you are wondering if I'm talking about you, I am.

CHAPTER ONE

A DIFFERENT WAY OF SERVING

"What am I supposed to do with a live turkey?" My dad and his cousin were at a singles dance, and between the two of them, they had "won" the door prize of a thanksgiving turkey. A live turkey. In a crate. Smelly. Loud. And alive.

The two young adults brainstormed ways to humanely get rid of the bird. Time has dimmed some of the specifics, but the details that Dad remembers are that a family (We'll call them the Wilsons) in his cousin's ward were struggling financially, but that they were too proud to accept charity. The two young men hatched a plan.

Dad said, "The Wilsons don't know me and won't recognize my voice. I'll call them and tell them they have won a prize. Maybe that'll be enough to get them to take the turkey." He picked up the phone and dialed the number. Scrambling to come up with a believable story when he heard Sister Wilson's sweet, "Hello," he said he was a radio DJ. "I'm calling to let you know that you have won a Thanksgiving turkey...IF you can answer three questions correctly."

Sister Wilson seemed a bit flustered. She didn't know if she could answer the questions right, but she would certainly try. I wish Dad could remember the questions that he asked the Wilsons, because he insists that the questions should have been easy. Things like 'What superhero does Clark Kent become?" or "Name a famous Kardashian." The one question he remembers is "What is the name of the Lone Ranger's horse."

Comic book aficionados and superhero fans alike would certainly know that the Lone Ranger's horse was named Silver. But, poor Sister Wilson didn't know the answer to *any* of the questions. She answered them all wrong! The Lone Ranger's horse? She thought that was his sidekick, Tonto.

Dad lied to Sister Wilson and enthusiastically announced after each incorrect response, "You are absolutely right!" After the third wrong answer in a row, he congratulated her for winning the Thanksgiving prize. "Our team will deliver the turkey later tonight."

They dropped off the crate on the Wilson's front porch and laughed at their antics. A couple of hours later, they drove by the Wilsons darkened home to see that Brother Wilson was hard at work plucking the bird under the lone porch light. They had effectively dumped the turkey. All was well.

Weeks, or maybe months later, Dad found out the rest of the story. Sister Wilson stood in Testimony Meeting and shared how God answered their prayer. She explained that they didn't have much, and they certainly wouldn't have enough to buy a Thanksgiving turkey that year. They cautioned their kids, who had been praying for a turkey, that God doesn't answer all prayers. Well, He does, but not always the ones we want.

Then, she explained, this nice man from the radio called and asked me some questions. "I don't know how I got the answers right, but I did, and somehow, we won a Thanksgiving turkey." God had answered the innocent prayers of her young children. Unintentionally, Dad and his cousin ended up at the right place, at the right time, doing the right thing. The result blessed the lives of a family in ways that they may never truly understand.

One of my best friends, CJ, is blind. He has told me that he can do just about anything that anyone else can do except see. (I confess that I won't let him drive my car, though.) One day, CJ texted me and suggested that we go to the ice cream place.

CJ lived about 15 minutes from me, so it was not particularly convenient to go to his house, pick him up, drive to Handel's Ice Cream (which is about halfway between our houses), take him back home, and then drive home. The Chocoholic Chunk ice cream, though, was almost always worth it. Of course, I had to sample a few different flavors first.

If I were ask you to think of a scripture that teaches about serving others, there's a very good chance that you would come up with Mosiah 2:17, "when ye are in the service of your fellow beings ye are only in the service of your God." That scripture is great! I jokingly offered to CJ that I would take him to Handel's any time he wants, because in driving him to get ice cream, according to that passage, I am actually serving God.

The best part of the scripture is that it's true. By serving others—*any* others—I really am serving God. By driving CJ to get ice cream, I am serving God. By dumping the Thanksgiving turkey off on the Wilsons, my dad was serving God.

We don't have to justify the type or quantify the amount of service we give. We just need to serve. Serve others. Any others. And we are serving God. King Benjamin said so, and I believe him.

THE CHOCOLATE CAKE PHENOMENON

CHAPTER TWO

THE REAL LANGUAGE GAP

"I Love you!" I remember awkwardly saying this to my wife for the first time. I remember saying it to my mom the other day at the end of our phone call. I wrote it in an email to my missionary daughter. I have even said it to co-workers, but with each person, the words—those exact same words—meant very different things. English (and probably most any other language) is woefully inadequate at conveying *experiences*. It's even just marginal at conveying meaning.

Here's what I mean. Imagine that you have a large piece of chocolate cake on a plate in front of you. You take a fork and push it through the thick frosting and the rich, dark cake to serve up a perfect bite-sized mouthful. You savor it. Chew, swallow, and rinse it down with a cold glass of chocolate milk. (If you're one of those weirdos who doesn't like chocolate cake, you'll have to try this thought experiment with kale chips or whatever else might excite you.)

Now, describe the experience in a way that gives your audience the same experience.

You might use words like "Decadent." "Moist." "Delicious." "Sweet." "Chocolatey." In any case, you may have conveyed some level of *meaning*, but it's unlikely that you effectively gave anyone else the same experience that you had while eating the cake.

Even if you and your audience both know what all of

those words mean, your description of your experience pales in comparison with the real experience. Try it. Try to describe an experience—any experience—with someone who hasn't had that exact experience in such a way that your description gives them the exact feelings, thoughts, and emotions of living that same experience. How does it feel to skydive? To water-ski? To see the birth of your first child? To mourn the loss of a loved one? What does it feel like when your stomach is so full of sushi that you can't shove another piece in?

The words are all there, but the *experience* can't effectively be shared. Even with true empathy, our language falls short of conveying an experience.

Look at Lehi's vision, for example. The way he describes the fruit of the tree changes after he partakes of the fruit. He saw the tree "whose fruit was desirable to make one happy." (1 Nephi 8:10) To me, Lehi seems to be observing a tree, and he somehow knows that the fruit is good. He logically understands that the fruit will make him happy, but hasn't tasted it yet. At this point, it's a belief.

Verses 11-12 show a different side of Lehi's experience with the fruit. He tasted it. It filled his soul with "exceedingly great joy." The fruit, as we learn in 1 Nephi 11, represents the love of God. I imagine that Lehi, at this point in his vision, *felt* the deep love that God has for him. He *felt* it, and his description of the fruit changed from "it was desirable to make one happy" to "it filled my soul with exceedingly great joy."

We can learn from Lehi that hearing about something, reading about it, thinking about it, watching someone else experience it, and so on, is not the same as having the experience ourselves. Ironically, I'm trying to convey my experience by sharing words, and I know that's not enough. So, I am asking you to understand two things: First, as you read about the rest of the Phenomenon, you will understand the words. You may empathize with the experiences. You may even know in your head that the

Chocolate Cake Phenomenon will work for you, and that you will see the blessings. That is all true.

So, second, I invite you to actually *do* the things that I have experienced. Try it out. Test it. See how it feels. See if my description is doing it justice.

Spoiler alert: My explanation can't even come close.

THE CHOCOLATE CAKE PHENOMENON

CHAPTER THREE

GOD LOVES HIS CHILDREN

E very six months it seems, I hear someone say in General Conference, "Heavenly Father loves *you*.". The way I like to understand it is, "He loves *you*, personally, individually, *you*." as opposed to "He loves all y'all."

Because I happen to know that this is true.

I was a new member of the High Council, and part of my stewardship over the Young Women's program allowed me to attend Girls' Camp. To set some context, Girls' Camp is very different than Scout Camp, and it's not just that the campers are female. The challenges that the campers face are different. The experiences that they have are different. Even the purposes of the camps are very different.

This was my first experience as a Priesthood holder serving at Girls' Camp. Part of my duties included being available to offer Priesthood blessings to anyone who needed or wanted a blessing for any reason. There were two of us, and we were called upon several times for a variety of needs. Homesickness, illness, and other typical requests.

For Thursday afternoon at 2:00, I had been asked to teach a mini class on ASL, American Sign Language. I was going to share with the girls a few signs and their meaning and teach them about how the hymn "High on a Mountain Top" teaches us about the temple.

The girls assigned to my class were gathered, and I was a few seconds from starting the class when the Assistant Camp Director called over to me. "Brother Williams, we have a young woman who needs a Priesthood blessing."

For a moment, I felt conflicted. I had a duty to offer blessings when they were needed and wanted. I also had, at this same exact time, a duty to teach a class. There were 40 girls waiting for me to begin. I knew the right thing was to find someone to cover the mini class, with no notice, and attend to the spiritual needs of the One. I found a couple of people, including my own daughter, to stall the class long enough for me to visit with the girl asking for a blessing.

You probably know people like this girl, who I will call Catherine. She was the weird kid. She was not popular. I deeply love her, but she was odd. I asked Catherine what was going on that she needed blessing, and her reason for asking for a blessing was a bit strange as well.

I thought, "There is a large group of girls waiting for me to start their class, *but, Catherine deserves my full attention.*" I pushed thoughts of the class aside and silently prayed that I would know what words I should offer in this blessing.

When I give a priesthood blessing, I don't get a script pushed into my brain with the words that I should say. Normally, I get impressions. I then have to figure out how to put those impressions into words. I put my hands on Catherine's head and started the blessing.

What happened next can not be explained in words. I don't have words to adequately share the depth or magnitude of what I felt. All I can say is I *felt* God's love. I *felt* how deeply she is loved. I caught a glimpse of how Heavenly Father feels about this precious daughter. ***I felt it.***

I then began suffering from the Real Language Gap. I couldn't put that feeling into any words other than "You are a *deeply* loved daughter of your Heavenly Father." Tears were streaming down my face. (If you have ever stood and said, "We are daughters of a Heavenly Father who loves us…" you should know that it is true. I know it because *I have felt it.*)

This is why I love the change in how Lehi describes the fruit, because I have felt it, too. The love of God will fill your soul with exceedingly great joy. It did for me.

CHAPTER FOUR

HE LOVES ME (AND YOU!)

Why was having faith not good enough for Nephi? For a long time, when I would discuss the scripture stories with Youth (I *love* asking questions that make people—and me—think) I would ask that question. We know that Nephi had faith, and after hearing about his father, Lehi's, dream, Nephi wanted to see the same vision. So, was it not good enough for Nephi to just believe the words of his father?

I remember pondering on a parallel question one sacrament meeting. The Thursday before, the Stake President shared about an experience he had in the temple. "I'm not going to tell you what I experienced, but when you go to the temple next time…" he then posed a question for us to ponder. The teaching moment was unique, and as a member of the High Council, I was fascinated with his style.

While the sacrament was being passed, I sat, reading 1 Nephi 10. Verse 17 hit me in a way it had never landed on me before: Nephi wanted to "see and hear and know" the things his father had seen and heard and known *because Nephi needed to have his own experience.* This wasn't a question of faith—it was the difference between Nephi just hearing about the fruit versus *tasting* the fruit. It was the same as reading a description of chocolate cake or eating it.

Wow! The Stake President was wise enough to not give us the answer to an insight he had. He wanted us to "see and hear and know" for ourselves the truths taught in the temple. His question focused our minds on a specific nugget. In the same way, it wasn't that Nephi didn't have faith in what his father's vision taught, but he wanted (and deserved) to have his own experience.

I don't remember what prompted my prayer. Maybe I was feeling invisible or forgotten. Maybe I was experiencing a low self-esteem moment. But I remember the night I wondered. I was a lot of years old, and for some reason, I was suddenly curious if Heavenly Father cared—or even knew who I was.

Sure, I knew He loved His children, and as one His children, that would likely include me. But it was that one night that I knelt down, wondering if He knew *me*.

I suspect not everyone will have the exact same experience that I had, but my experience made it very clear that yes, He knows who I am. He knows me. He knows *me*. I am one of His children, and he loves *me*. For me the feeling was instant and unmistakable, and it brought me to tears.

I *know* He loves *me*.

My daughter had a different path to the same experience. She can't talk about it. I suspect it's because there are no words. She told me that she prayed as a young woman to know if Heavenly Father knows who she is.

Nothing…She felt nothing.

Continued prayer brought nothing more. But then, during a Young Women class lesson, she was reading an article from a recent General Conference address. I don't think it really matters who wrote the talk or what the speaker said, but as she read it, she *felt* it. She knew. She was overcome with the feeling of love that God has for *her*. She is one of His children. He knows *her*. She tasted the fruit.

As a father, there is no lesson more important that I

can think of than for one of my children to discover how He feels about her. It is my wish that all of my children can know how their Heavenly Father feels about them.

I learned two things. Foremost, if He feels "that way" about me, and he feels the same way about Catherine, and he feels the same way about my sweet daughter, I *know* He feels the same way about *you*. Yes, you are a deeply loved child of God. He loves *you*.

If he loves me, and Catherine, and my daughter, and you this deeply, shouldn't we do anything we can to be kind to His children?

THE CHOCOLATE CAKE PHENOMENON

KEN WILLIAMS

CHAPTER FIVE

THOSE COOKIES ARE NOT FOR YOU

The sweet smell of freshly baked chocolate chip cookies hit as I entered the house after a long workday. A stack of warm and soft, perfectly browned cookies was on the counter. At the marginal risk of losing my dinner appetite, I reached out to take one.

My wife slapped my hand away. She literally slapped my hand!

"Those are not for you!"

Perfectly baked chocolate chip cookies are among the best foods in the world, and I could not imagine a scenario that would include cookies in my kitchen that I was not allowed to eat. I whimpered, "Who are they for, then?"

"The Browns."

"What's going on with the Browns that you're making cookies for them?" My sweetheart was the Compassionate Service leader, and I was accustomed to her making entire meals for families who had a need. Her answer was unexpected.

"I don't know. I just felt like they needed cookies."

Mind. Blown. This made no sense to me, so I let it pass by. I would somehow have to survive the night without a cookie. And they looked like the perfect combination of soft and crisp.

I put the experience out of mind until a few weeks later when Sister Brown called and left a message on voicemail. "I just wanted to thank you for the cookies the other day. That was *exactly what we needed.*"

I didn't know how to process that, so I left the entire experience on the back burner.

Sometime later, I came home from work to see six canning jars lined up on the counter. They were half-full of water, and each donned a simple bow. Black-eyed Susans from the front garden were neatly arranged in each jar.

"Cool flowers. Who are they for," I asked my wife.

The answer gave me a flashback to the Browns and the forbidden cookies. Her sweet reply was, "Hmm... I don't know."

At the start of our date that evening, she explained that a sister in the ward had just lost her mother. "We'll deliver one bouquet to Sister Stevens. Where should we go after that?"

The question first startled me. *How am I supposed to know who we should take flowers to?* But a name popped into my mind. My home teaching family. I could have easily said with confidence, "Let's take some to the Thompsons." But, for reasons I can't now fathom, I felt afraid to commit. "I don't know who to take them to," was my weak reply.

My wife thought for a moment and said, "Let's take some to the Thompsons." The coincidence was startling. I later realized that there was no coincidence.

We pulled up to the Thompson's house and we saw them in the front yard. My wife took the flowers to Sister Thompson and began a friendly chat. Brother Thompson was busy unloading construction debris: bricks, bags of concrete, and rocks, from a wooden pallet in the middle of the driveway. I walked over and began helping.

"Someone dumped this pallet of bricks in the middle of our driveway," Brother Thompson fumed. It was clear that there were several ongoing construction projects in the neighborhood. "We can't figure out who did it, and no one will claim responsibility, but we can't get our cars in or out of the garage until it is moved." A few minutes later, we had the driveway cleared, and Brother Thompson seemed much less stressed.

But it wasn't until later that I recognized that the Thompson's name popping into my head was a spiritual prompting.

THE CHOCOLATE CAKE PHENOMENON

CHAPTER SIX

HE KNOWS WHERE HIS CHILDREN ARE

My oldest son, we'll call him David, has decided that the path he wants to follow does not currently include the Church of Jesus Christ. This is uncharted territory for me, and I have been cautious not to withhold love or fellowship. He is our son regardless of the decisions he makes—or even whether we agree or disagree with them.

I don't know if I am praying the right way or for the right thing, but my constant prayer has been that he will have the experiences that he needs in order to draw closer to Jesus Christ. There are things that I, in my own almost-infinite wisdom, think should happen.

David announced during the spring that he would be leaving his home state and moving to California for a summer job. He would be working with his cousin, and we felt that the association would be good for him. His road trip out West would take him through Utah, also, where his sister is serving as a missionary on Temple Square. "And," David decided, "I think I will stop by Temple Square and visit my sister.

I had high hopes for this meeting. Being in a place where he could feel the spirit would be great for him. Visiting with his sister would be positive. She certainly exudes the Light of Christ, and she is a beautiful example of charity. (In fairness, I should say that of all the Temple Square sisters I have met have these same qualities.)

However, I also knew that the scheduling of Temple Square sisters may not neatly coincide with David's planned visit. I prayed that they would connect, and I imagined that their meeting should follow a specific schedule of events for both to be edified according to my desires.

Friday afternoon at 4:00, I received a call from David. "I'm a few minutes out from Temple Square. I'll be there shortly." He just wanted me to know his whereabouts, and I coached him on how he could most likely connect with his sister. I explained that I wanted to hear the outcome, but I would be unavailable for the next several hours. I knew I could only wait, so I offered a final silent prayer that their paths would cross in my pre-conceived way.

I don't have dramatic spiritual impression often, but as I readied for my 5:00 commitment, I felt a very paternal comfort accompanying the words, *"Heavenly Father knows where His children are."*

I instantly knew David was in good hands. Better hands than mine. I was at peace, but I was also excited to hear how the brother/sister meeting went.

Several hours later and after several conversations, I pieced together the event. David was walking on Temple Square and he saw his aunt.

That's right. *My* sister was visiting Temple Square from Seattle, Washington. They were rounding out their spring break and college visits with a quick trip to Temple Square. My sister was hopeful that she, too, would "bump into" my daughter. They did. As they approached the flagpole where the tours normally start, they saw her familiar face.

At almost the same time, David recognized his aunt. (He has changed enough in the years since she has seen him that it took her a few minutes to notice him)

David, his sister, and his aunt and cousins all "happened" to show up on Temple Square at the same exact moment. What are the chances of that?

Elder Bednar has said that there are no coincidences in the gospel of Jesus Christ. The chances of those three connecting the way they did is zero. But they did. Heavenly Father knows where His children are.

And the greatest thing for me is that the little family reunion that He orchestrated was so much better than whatever I had in mind.

I was involved in a project at work many years ago, and the project required that the participants be focused on the steps along the way. That meant no time off for the foreseeable future.

At the same time, my grandmother's health was declining. She was living with my parents, and we would get regular updates on Grandma's condition. "She's not getting out of bed much anymore," or "She is tired all the time."

One Wednesday morning the project leader announced that the loose ends were wrapping up within the next two days. We could start to take time off! I felt a compelling urge to make a final visit to see Grandma. Everything fell into place, and I flew to California two days later—without telling anyone that I was coming.

Friday evening, I knocked on the door of my childhood home, but there was no answer. I knew Grandma wasn't leaving; therefore, a caretaker would certainly be there. I knocked harder.

My mom answered in shock. "What are you doing here?" I came up with some lame joke about getting lost and needing directions. I spent the next few days enjoying the company of my parents, a couple of aunts, and two very brief visits with Grandma. She was too weak to spend more than five minutes or so with me.

I returned home on Thursday and Grandma died on Friday. For years, I attributed the urging I felt to visit Grandma to the timing of her passing. Until my mom asked my wife if she had ever shared the rest of the story. She had not.

My dad had a trip planned to Seattle to visit my sister. He left Friday morning—the same Friday when I arrived in the evening. The night before, Dad gave his mother a blessing and gave her permission to prepare to pass through the veil. Then he left.

My sweet mother was afflicted with levels of stress that I can only imagine. She had great faith, but she felt very vulnerable taking care of her mother-in-law, who was surely going to pass soon. And her husband was away. She felt like she needed someone with the Priesthood in the home to be a comfort. She prayed that somehow, she could have a Priesthood holder in her home. Then Dad left. Her prayer seemed to be unanswered. Then I coincidentally showed up.

Dad was only gone a couple of days, and I didn't do anything special, but my presence offered support and comfort. And I didn't even know it.

Heavenly Father knows where His children are. And he will direct their—and our—paths, if we will let Him.

CHAPTER SEVEN

THE CHOCOLATE CAKE
PHENOMENON

My birthday is in November (you don't have to send cards, but it would be totally cool if you did), and before I started making my own birthday cakes, I would go to the local big warehouse club store each year and buy a multi-layer very big chocolate cake. It was quite delicious, but after eating a couple of pieces, I was pretty much done.

Then the cake would sit on the counter. I had a choice. I could let it go bad (does cake go bad? It would dry out, I guess and get stale. I suppose that's the same as going bad) or I could share with people I knew who liked chocolate cake.

Fortunately, I know several people who like chocolate cake. I make mental notes when I learn what people's likes and dislikes are, and I have accumulated a list of people who would not be opposed to helping me finish a portion of my birthday cake.

One year, several days after my birthday, I cut a couple hunks of cake, foil wrapped the plates, and set out on a cake-delivery mission. I had two destinations in mind, and the first was a large family in the ward. I was pretty sure that they would not object to a surprise visit with a plateful of cake. I made the short drive to their home, took a plate of velvety goodness, and knocked on the door.

I waited. No answer. I knocked again. Harder.

The Sprit prompted me in a different direction. **You**

need to visit your home teaching family. *I'll swing by their house next,* I thought.

I could hear movement behind the door. I rang the doorbell. Still no answer. The thought returned. **Go see your home teaching family**

Yeah, yeah, I thought. *Right after I drop the cake off here.*

I picked up my cell phone and dialed their number.

No answer. **Visit your home teaching family.**

I finally recognized the Spirit. *I think I'll go visit my home teaching family.* I abandoned the effort to deliver the cake, and I drove the short distance to my home teaching family. Not wanting a perfectly good chunk of cake to be wasted, and since the original family wasn't answering, I walked to the door with the plate in hand. When Sister Thompson answered the door, I held it out. "The Spirit told me I should bring you chocolate cake." I thought I was being clever.

Sister Thompson absently took the cake as she invited me in. She thanked me for coming and explained, "Our infant son is sick and needs a blessing. Can you help my husband administer to him?"

I instantly realized why the prompting came so forcefully as I was standing on the other family's front porch. They didn't need cake nearly as much as the family I was assigned to minister to needed a blessing. I was humbled, and I agreed to help with the blessing.

I was a fairly new Stake Young Men's president counseling with a ward Young Men's president. He wasn't convinced that his calling was inspired. "I'm the president only because no one else will do it." He didn't even like the calling.

I'm sure that's possible, but I could hardly imagine not wanting to serve in a calling that works with Youth. And it wasn't like the ward was big. He oversaw a program that served seven boys. Two of them were his own sons.

I struggled to come up with some wisdom that would have an impact on how he served. Instead, I gained an insight that changed how I serve. I heard myself ask the reluctant president if he would try something for me.

"Yeah, I guess. What is it?"

"I want you to pray for your young men every day for one week. By name.

"That's it?" It must have seemed too simple.

"That's it."

I listened to my own advice and started praying for my stewardship by name every day. I have no idea how it affected his calling, but it made a world of difference in mine.

Shortly after this experience, I was called to serve as the Seminary teacher. I had 19 students, and I was intimidated. I knew the impact that a Seminary teacher could have—or not have. I began praying for them every day. By name.

Occasionally, a name would catch in my mind during my prayer. It was almost like a speed bump. And my heavenward plea wasn't elaborate; I would ask Heavenly Father to bless Tony, and please bless Maggie, and please bless Aubrey, and bless Heather. That was it, but sometimes I felt the need to pay close attention to one of the students.

I had some leftover brownies (hard to believe that there is such a thing as leftover brownies, but somehow, I had them) on a Sunday evening. During that morning's prayer, I had caught on Nathan's name. I drove to Nathan's house and knocked on the door. His father answered and invited me in. He called Nathan down from his room.

"Hey, I have a couple of questions for you," I started when Nathan entered the room. He looked at me suspiciously. I asked, "How's Seminary going?"

He looked at his feet. "Not very well. I haven't been very reverent lately."

We had a short but heartfelt chat, where I invited him

to prepare a message for the class, and he told me he would be willing to improve his reverence. I left feeling like the time was well spent. He later told me the impact of this visit.

After several such visits, I recognized that a consistent pattern was developing. Prayer led to spiritual promptings, and when I acted on them, I ended up serving individuals who benefitted in various ways. After each visit, I felt enriched and inspired. Regardless of the immediate outcome, I left feeling blessed. And *sometimes* I learned that my simple act of service was especially meaningful.

A seminary student told me that my visit with a plate of cookies was "exactly what I needed." A member of the ward told me when I stopped by that the visit was "an answer to prayer." One family told me several years later that the timing of the cake delivery was particularly meaningful. "We just moved here and didn't know anyone. And we were experiencing a difficult medical situation. And you showed up with chocolate cake."

Being at the right place at the right time to bless other people's lives is *The Chocolate Cake Phenomenon.*

CHAPTER EIGHT

WHO DO I KNOW WHO NEEDS CHOCOLATE CAKE?

My logic may not resonate with everyone, but I tend to think that sharing chocolate cake with others is a good thing. Recognizing and acting on promptings of the Spirit is good. Being prompted to share cake with someone and then taking cake to them is good.

Moroni 7:13 teaches that *"every thing* which inviteth and enticeth to do good…" is inspired of God. And verse 16 reinforces that we can know "with a perfect knowledge" that things which invite us to do good are inspired.

Therefore, if you receive a prompting to share chocolate cake with someone, that is inspired. Heavenly Father will tell you who needs chocolate cake. Ask, and ye shall receive.

And there's no required schedule. I discovered that I didn't have to wait until I had leftovers. I could make cake any time, ponder on who I know who needs cake, and then make a delivery. I can do this any time.

I have been able to involve others in the process. I have asked my kids who they know who needs chocolate cake. The Lord answers them, too. Then, after we make a visit, I ask my kids what made them think of the person we had just visited. Sometimes there is a clear reason, and sometimes it's more nebulous, but I can usually teach my kids that their answer is the result of the Spirit prompting them.

So, instead of waiting for leftovers, I make cake and a visit on any schedule I want. For me, Sunday evenings are a good time. I might make a cake or three on a Sunday afternoon, then I ponder on who needs it. Sometimes I'll get a feeling as someone walks past me at church. Maybe I have heard some news that keeps someone on my mind. Sometimes, a name pops into my head from out of the blue. It doesn't matter.

Occasionally, I feel a bit of anxiety because I'm not sure how people will receive the visit. Maybe I don't know them well, or I know they're dealing with devastating news. Interestingly, I have never been turned away. Almost always, the moments of anxiety are greatly overshadowed by a calming comfort that we visited the right friend.

Sometimes, I'll be on my way to visit one family and another family's name will crowd out the first. I've learned to act on the new prompting. Heavenly Father knows His children, and He knows who needs chocolate cake.

Chocolate cake visits are wonderful. They may be short or long. On the front porch or in the living room. I love them all, and I am never disappointed. I don't have any agenda other than to share. My role, I've decided, is to make and deliver cake. I'm not trying to be the answer to prayer or to change anyone's life. But sometimes I learn that my visit is the answer to prayer or that it did change someone's life.

And it doesn't have to be chocolate cake. It works with chocolate chip cookies. Or cinnamon rolls. Or flowers. Or zucchini bread. Or fresh garden salsa. Or anything you have to share.

Follow the pattern. It works, and it blesses lives. Starting with your own.

KEN WILLIAMS

CHAPTER NINE

KEN'S MOM'S CHOCOALTE CAKE RECIPE

Ken's Mom's Chocolate Cake

Dutch processed cocoa powder will make a darker and richer cake. Buttermilk can be substituted with regular milk or sour milk. The secret ingredient, of course, is love and some butter.

In a saucepan boil:

2 sticks	butter
1 cup	water

Pour boiling ingredients over:

2 cups	Flour	½ tsp	Salt
2 cups	Sugar	1 tsp	Vanilla
1 tsp	Baking Soda	4 TBSP	Cocoa Powder
½ cup	Buttermilk	2	Eggs

Directions:

Mix ingredients together until smooth. Pour into a greased 9x13 pan. Bake at 350° for 30 minutes or until done.

Frosting:

Melt 1 stick butter with 5 TBSP buttermilk. Pour over 3 ½ to 4 cups powdered sugar, 1 tsp. vanilla, and 4 TBSP cocoa powder. Frost cake while still warm.

ABOUT THE AUTHOR

Ken Williams has been happily married to the same woman since 1990, and he is the father of five children. He is a published author, an amazing teacher, and one of the nicest people you'll ever meet. He is an expert at making chocolate cake, and he has the recipe memorized. Ken is the author of the Amazon best-selling business books 21 Days to Success through Networking and 21 Days to Success with LinkedIn as well as the less-than-helpful grammar book, Irregardless, and the real-life Christmas story, The Christmas Clock. You should probably buy them all.

Made in the USA
Coppell, TX
02 October 2020